From Text to Code, From Speech to Action

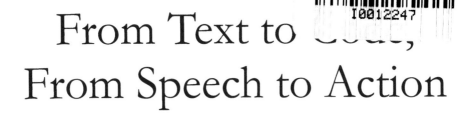

The Power of Natural Language Processing

Benjamin Evans

DEDICATION

To the relentless seekers of knowledge, the curious minds tirelessly decoding the mysteries of algorithms and code. This book is dedicated to you, the coders who embrace the challenges of neural networks with fervor and determination. May these pages serve as stepping stones on your journey, empowering you to unravel the complexities of this dynamic field and craft solutions that shape the future. Your passion fuels the innovation that drives our world forward, and for that, I extend my deepest gratitude and admiration.

CONTENTS

ACKNOWLEDGMENTS

I would like to extend my sincere gratitude to all those who have contributed to the realization of this book. First and foremost, I am indebted to my family for their unwavering support and encouragement throughout this endeavor. Their love and understanding have been my anchor in the stormy seas of writing.

I am deeply thankful to the experts whose guidance and insights have illuminated my path and enriched the content of this book. Their mentorship has been invaluable in shaping my understanding and refining my ideas.

I also extend my appreciation to those whose constructive feedback and insightful suggestions have helped polish this work to its finest form.

Furthermore, I am grateful to the countless individuals whose research, publications, and contributions have paved the way for the insights shared in these pages.

Last but not least, I express my heartfelt appreciation to the readers who embark on this journey with me. Your curiosity and engagement breathe life into these words, and it is for you that this book exists.

Thank you all for being part of this remarkable journey.

CHAPTER 1

Introduction to NLP

1.1: What is Natural Language Processing (NLP)?

Natural Language Processing (NLP) is a field of artificial intelligence (AI) that deals with the interaction between computers and human language. It aims to bridge the gap between how humans communicate and how machines process information. In simpler terms, NLP empowers computers to understand, analyze, and generate human language in a way that mimics human intelligence.

Here's a breakdown of what NLP entails:

- **Understanding:**
  - NLP techniques allow computers to extract meaning from text and speech. This includes tasks like sentiment analysis (identifying positive, negative, or neutral opinions), topic modeling (discovering the main themes in a document), and named entity recognition

(finding and classifying named entities like people, organizations, and locations).

- **Analysis:**
  - Once the meaning is extracted, NLP can analyze the language for various purposes. This could involve tasks like question answering (providing answers to user queries based on a given text corpus), text summarization (creating a concise summary of a longer piece of text), and machine translation (converting text from one language to another).

- **Generation:**
  - NLP can also be used to generate human-like text. This includes tasks like chatbots (conversational agents that simulate human interaction), text-to-speech synthesis (converting written text into spoken language), and creative writing (generating different kinds of creative text formats).

1.2: A Brief History of NLP

The roots of NLP can be traced back to the early days of

artificial intelligence in the 1950s. Pioneering work included machine translation systems and attempts to develop programs that could understand natural language questions.

Here are some key milestones in NLP history:

- **1950s:** The first machine translation systems are developed, with limited success.
- **1960s:** Research focuses on computational linguistics, analyzing the structure of language.
- **1970s:** Early natural language understanding systems are developed, with limitations in handling complex language.
- **1980s:** Expert systems using NLP techniques gain popularity in specific domains like medicine and finance.
- **1990s:** Statistical methods for NLP start to emerge, leading to improvements in tasks like speech recognition and machine translation.
- **2000s:** The rise of the internet fuels the growth of NLP applications with massive amounts of text data available.
- **2010s:** Deep learning revolutionizes NLP, achieving

breakthroughs in tasks like text classification, question answering, and machine translation.

- **Present Day:** NLP continues to evolve, with research focusing on areas like dialogue systems, explainable AI, and handling low-resource languages.

1.3: Why is NLP Important?

NLP plays a crucial role in bridging the communication gap between humans and machines. Here's why it's important:

- **Unlocks the Power of Big Data:** The vast amount of textual information available online (e.g., social media posts, news articles, customer reviews) becomes usable with NLP. This data can be analyzed for insights, trends, and patterns.

- **Improves Human-Computer Interaction:** NLP allows computers to understand user intent and respond in a natural and engaging way. This enhances user experience with applications like chatbots, virtual assistants, and search engines.

- **Automates Tasks:** NLP automates repetitive

text-based tasks such as document classification, data extraction, and sentiment analysis. This frees up human resources for more complex activities.

- **Personalized Experiences:** NLP personalized user experiences by analyzing preferences and tailoring content, recommendations, and interactions.

- **Breaks Down Language Barriers:** Machine translation powered by NLP allows for communication and information access across different languages.

1.4: Applications of NLP in Everyday Life

NLP applications are woven into the fabric of our everyday lives. Here are some examples:

- **Smartphones:** Voice assistants like Siri and Google Assistant use NLP for speech recognition and natural language understanding to respond to user queries and instructions.

- **Social Media:** NLP powers features like sentiment analysis to understand public opinion on trending topics and spam filtering to identify and remove unwanted content.

- **Email Services:** Spam filters utilize NLP techniques to identify and filter out unwanted emails based on their content.

- **Customer Service Chatbots:** NLP allows chatbots to understand customer inquiries and provide helpful responses or route them to human agents for complex issues.

- **Search Engines:** Search engines use NLP to understand user search queries and retrieve relevant results based on the meaning and context of the query.

- **Machine Translation Tools:** Services like Google Translate leverage NLP to translate text from one language to another, enabling communication across language barriers.

Code Snippet (Example - Sentiment Analysis using Python Library NLTK):

```
from          nltk.sentiment.vader          import
SentimentIntensityAnalyzer
```

```
# Sample text
text = "This movie was absolutely terrible. The acting
```

was awful, and the plot was nonsensical."

```
# Initialize SentimentIntensityAnalyzer
analyzer = SentimentIntensityAnalyzer()

# Analyze the sentiment of the text
sentiment = analyzer.polarity_scores(text)

# Print the sentiment scores
print(sentiment)
```

This code snippet demonstrates sentiment analysis using the NLTK library in Python.

CHAPTER 2

CORE CONCEPTS IN NLP

This chapter dives into the fundamental building blocks of NLP, exploring how language is structured, represented, and analyzed by machines.

2.1: Language Fundamentals: Morphology, Syntax, Semantics

Understanding the basic building blocks of language is crucial for NLP. Here's a breakdown of three key aspects:

- **Morphology:** Morphology deals with the structure of words and how they are formed. It focuses on morphemes, the smallest units of meaning in a language. For example, the word "unbreakable" is composed of three morphemes: "un-" (negation), "break" (verb root), and "-able" (suffix indicating possibility).
- **Syntax:** Syntax focuses on the grammatical structure of a sentence, how words are arranged to form

meaningful phrases and clauses. It defines the rules that govern word order and sentence formation. For example, the sentence "The cat chased the mouse" has a different meaning than "The mouse chased the cat" due to the different syntactic order of the words.

- **Semantics:** Semantics deals with the meaning of words and sentences. It goes beyond the individual words to understand the overall meaning conveyed by a sentence. This includes aspects like word sense disambiguation (identifying the intended meaning of a word based on context) and reference resolution (understanding which entity a pronoun refers to).

2.2: Text Representation: Bag-of-Words, Word Embeddings

When computers process text, they need a way to represent it numerically. Here are two common approaches:

- **Bag-of-Words (BoW):** This is a simple method that represents a document as a collection of words. Each word is treated independently, and its frequency in the document is counted. The BoW model ignores the order of words and grammatical structure.

Code Snippet (Example - Bag-of-Words using Python library scikit-learn):

```python
from sklearn.feature_extraction.text import CountVectorizer

# Sample documents
documents = ["This is a great movie", "The acting was superb", "But the plot was a bit predictable"]

# Create a CountVectorizer object
vectorizer = CountVectorizer()

# Fit the vectorizer to the documents
X = vectorizer.fit_transform(documents)

# Print the vocabulary and document-term matrix
print(vectorizer.get_feature_names_out())
print(X.toarray())
```

This code demonstrates how to create a Bag-of-Words representation for a set of documents using scikit-learn in Python.

- **Word Embeddings:** This method goes beyond simply counting word occurrences. Word embeddings represent words as vectors in a high-dimensional space, where words with similar meanings are positioned close together. This captures semantic relationships between words and allows for more nuanced text representation. Popular word embedding techniques include Word2Vec and GloVe.

2.3: Machine Learning for NLP: Supervised vs. Unsupervised Learning

Machine learning plays a central role in NLP tasks. Here's a breakdown of two main learning paradigms:

- **Supervised Learning:** In supervised learning, the model learns from labeled data. This data consists of text examples and their corresponding labels (e.g., sentiment labels for sentiment analysis, topic labels for topic modeling). The model learns to map the input text to the desired output based on the training data. Examples of supervised learning algorithms used in NLP include Support Vector Machines

(SVMs), Random Forests, and Gradient Boosting.

Code Snippet (Example - Sentiment Analysis using Supervised Learning with scikit-learn):

```
from sklearn.model_selection import train_test_split
from sklearn.linear_model import LogisticRegression

# Sample data with sentiment labels
data = [("This movie was awesome!", "positive"), ("The acting was terrible", "negative"), ...]

# Split data into training and testing sets
X_train, X_test, y_train, y_test = train_test_split(data[:, 0], data[:, 1])

# Vectorize the text data (e.g., using Word2Vec)
# ... (vectorization code)

# Train a Logistic Regression model for sentiment classification
model = LogisticRegression()
model.fit(X_train, y_train)
```

```
# Evaluate the model's performance on the test set
# ... (evaluation code)
```

This code snippet illustrates a basic supervised learning approach for sentiment analysis using scikit-learn.

- **Unsupervised Learning (Continued):** Examples of unsupervised learning algorithms used in NLP include K-Means clustering (grouping similar documents together) and Latent Dirichlet Allocation (LDA) for topic modeling (discovering the main themes in a collection of documents).

2.4: Evaluation Metrics for NLP Tasks

Evaluating the performance of NLP models is crucial to assess their effectiveness. Here are some common metrics used for different NLP tasks:

- **Classification Tasks (e.g., sentiment analysis, spam filtering):**
  - **Accuracy:** The proportion of correctly classified examples.
  - **Precision:** The proportion of true positives among predicted positives (avoiding false

positives).

- ○ **Recall:** The proportion of true positives identified by the model (avoiding false negatives).
- ○ **F1-score:** A harmonic mean of precision and recall, combining both metrics.

- **Regression Tasks (e.g., sentiment intensity scoring):**
  - ○ **Mean Squared Error (MSE):** The average squared difference between predicted and actual values.
  - ○ **Root Mean Squared Error (RMSE):** The square root of MSE, measured in the same units as the data.

- **Ranking Tasks (e.g., search engine ranking):**
  - ○ **Mean Average Precision (MAP):** Measures the average precision at each relevant document retrieved.
  - ○ **Normalized Discounted Cumulative Gain (NDCG):** Evaluates the ranking quality based

on the graded relevance of retrieved documents.

- **Clustering Tasks (e.g., topic modeling):**
  - ○ **Silhouette Coefficient:** Measures how well individual data points are assigned to their clusters.
  - ○ **Calinski-Harabasz Index:** Compares the average within-cluster distance to the between-cluster distance.

Additional Considerations:

- The choice of evaluation metric depends on the specific NLP task and the desired outcome.
- Human evaluation is often used alongside automated metrics to assess the quality and naturalness of NLP outputs (e.g., generated text, machine translation).

By understanding these core concepts and techniques, you'll gain a solid foundation for exploring the exciting world of NLP!

CHAPTER 3

NATURAL LANGUAGE UNDERSTANDING (NLU)

Natural Language Understanding (NLU) is a subfield of NLP that focuses on extracting meaning from human language. It aims to bridge the gap between how humans communicate and how machines interpret that communication. This chapter explores some of the key NLU tasks and techniques.

3.1: Text Classification: Sentiment Analysis, Topic Modeling

Text classification involves assigning text data to predefined categories. Here are two common types of text classification tasks:

a) Sentiment Analysis:

Sentiment analysis aims to identify the emotional tone or opinion expressed in a piece of text. It categorizes text into sentiments like positive, negative, or neutral. This can be applied to analyze customer reviews, social media posts, or product descriptions.

Code Snippet (Example - Sentiment Analysis using NLTK):

```python
import nltk
from nltk.sentiment.vader import SentimentIntensityAnalyzer

# Sample text
text = "This movie was a total disappointment. The acting was awful, and the plot was nonsensical."

# Initialize SentimentIntensityAnalyzer
analyzer = SentimentIntensityAnalyzer()

# Analyze the sentiment of the text
sentiment = analyzer.polarity_scores(text)

# Print the sentiment scores (positive, negative, neutral, and compound score)
print(sentiment)
```

b) Topic Modeling:

Topic modeling discovers the underlying thematic structure of a collection of documents. It identifies a set of topics that best represent the content and categorizes documents based on these topics. This is useful for analyzing news articles, research papers, or customer feedback to understand the main themes discussed.

Code Snippet (Example - Topic Modeling using scikit-learn):

```python
from sklearn.decomposition import LatentDirichletAllocation

# Sample documents (preprocessed text)
documents = [
    "This document talks about machine learning algorithms.",
    "This document discusses natural language processing techniques.",
    "..." # More documents
]

# Create a LatentDirichletAllocation model
lda_model = LatentDirichletAllocation(n_topics=5,
```

```
random_state=0)


    # Fit the model to the documents
    lda_model.fit(documents)


    # Print the topics discovered by the model
    for            topic_idx,            topic            in
enumerate(lda_model.components_):
        print(f"Topic {topic_idx + 1}:", [word for word, prob
in    sorted(zip(lda_model.features_[topic_idx],    topic),
reverse=True)[:5]])
```

This code snippet demonstrates topic modeling with Latent Dirichlet Allocation (LDA) using scikit-learn.

3.2: Named Entity Recognition (NER) and Relation Extraction

a) Named Entity Recognition (NER):

Named Entity Recognition (NER) identifies and classifies named entities in text data. These entities can be people, organizations, locations, dates, monetary values, etc. NER helps extract structured information from text, making it

19

valuable for tasks like information retrieval and question answering.

Code Snippet (Example - Named Entity Recognition using spaCy):

```python
import spacy

# Load the spaCy English language model
nlp = spacy.load("en_core_web_sm")

# Sample text
text = "Barack Obama, the former president of the United States, visited Paris, France in 2018."

# Process the text with spaCy
doc = nlp(text)

# Iterate over named entities and print their labels and text
for entity in doc.ents:
    print(entity.label_, entity.text)
```

This code snippet demonstrates NER with spaCy, a popular NLP library in Python.

b) Relation Extraction:

Relation extraction builds upon NER by identifying relationships between named entities. It aims to understand how entities are connected and what actions or events are described in the text. This can be used to create knowledge graphs or analyze social networks.

3.3: Text Summarization: Extractive vs. Abstractive Summarization

Text summarization aims to create a concise version of a longer piece of text while preserving the key information and meaning. There are two main approaches:

a) Extractive Summarization:

Extractive summarization identifies the most important sentences from the original text and combines them to form a summary. It often uses techniques like sentence scoring based on factors like word frequency or position to select the most relevant sentences.

b) Abstractive Summarization:

Abstractive summarization goes beyond simply extracting sentences. It aims to understand the main points and generate a new, shorter text that conveys the essential meaning of the original text. This requires a deeper understanding of language and often utilizes machine learning techniques like recurrent neural networks (RNNs).

3.4: Question Answering Systems: Extractive and Generative Approaches

Question Answering Systems (QAS) aim to answer user questions based on a given text corpus. Here are two main approaches:

a) Extractive Question Answering:

Extractive QAS systems identify the answer to a question by searching the text corpus for relevant keywords or phrases. They then extract sentences or passages that contain these keywords and present them as the answer. This approach is efficient but may not always provide the most comprehensive or informative answer.

b) Generative Question Answering:

Generative QAS systems go beyond keyword matching. They utilize advanced machine learning models, particularly transformer architectures like BERT, to understand the context and semantics of the question and the text corpus. These models can then generate a new answer sentence that directly addresses the user's query, even if the answer isn't explicitly stated in the text.

Code Snippet (Example - Simple Rule-based Extractive QAS with NLTK):

```python
import nltk

# Sample question and text passage
question = "What is the capital of France?"
passage = "France is a country located in Western Europe. Paris is the capital of France and one of the most popular tourist destinations in the world."

# Tokenize the passage
tokens = nltk.word_tokenize(passage)

# Lowercase the question and tokens for case-insensitive matching
```

```
lower_question = question.lower()
lower_tokens = [token.lower() for token in tokens]


# Find sentences containing answer keywords (e.g.,
"capital", "France")
answer_sentences = [sentence for sentence in
nltk.sent_tokenize(passage) if any(word in lower_tokens
for word in ["capital", "france"])]


# Print the first answer sentence as the answer
if answer_sentences:
  print(answer_sentences[0])
else:
  print("Answer not found in the passage.")
```

Note: This is a simplified example of an extractive QAS system. More sophisticated techniques involve ranking sentences based on relevance to the question.

By exploring these NLU tasks and techniques, we gain insights into how machines can understand the nuances of human language and extract valuable information from text data.

CHAPTER 4

SPEECH RECOGNITION AND NATURAL LANGUAGE GENERATION (NLG)

This chapter delves into two fundamental aspects of human-computer interaction: understanding spoken language (speech recognition) and generating human-like text (natural language generation).

4.1: Automatic Speech Recognition (ASR): From Acoustics to Text

Automatic Speech Recognition (ASR) transforms spoken language into computer-understandable text. Here's a breakdown of the process:

- **Acoustic Feature Extraction:** The first step involves converting the analog speech signal into a digital representation. Then, features like Mel-Frequency Cepstral Coefficients (MFCCs) are extracted. These features capture the spectral characteristics of the speech signal, representing the frequency content at different points in time.

- **Acoustic Modeling:** An acoustic model maps the extracted features to a sequence of phonemes (the basic units of sound in a language). This model is typically trained on a large corpus of speech data with corresponding phonetic transcriptions.

- **Language Modeling:** A language model predicts the most likely sequence of words given the sequence of phonemes recognized by the acoustic model. This incorporates knowledge of grammar, syntax, and word probabilities to improve accuracy.

- **Decoding:** The final stage combines the acoustic and language models to produce the most likely word sequence representing the spoken utterance. Techniques like beam search are used to efficiently search for the optimal sequence.

Code Snippet (Example - Feature Extraction with Librosa in Python):

```
import librosa

# Load an audio file
y, sr = librosa.load("your_audio_file.wav")
```

```
# Extract Mel-Frequency Cepstral Coefficients (MFCCs)
mfccs = librosa.feature.mfcc(y=y, sr=sr)


# Print the shape of the MFCCs matrix (features, time steps)
print(mfccs.shape)
```

4.2: Speaker Recognition and Diarization

- **Speaker Recognition:** This technology identifies the speaker of a spoken utterance. It analyzes voice characteristics like pitch, timbre, and speaking style to distinguish different speakers. This can be used for applications like voice authentication or personalized voice assistants.

- **Diarization:** This task involves segmenting a multi-speaker audio recording and identifying who spoke each segment. This is beneficial for tasks like analyzing group conversations or meetings.

4.3: Text-to-Speech Synthesis (TTS): Creating Natural-Sounding Speech

Text-to-Speech Synthesis (TTS) converts written text into spoken language. It aims to generate natural-sounding speech that mimics human pronunciation, intonation, and prosody. Here's a simplified view of the process:

- **Text Preprocessing:** The text is first preprocessed to handle factors like punctuation, abbreviations, and proper nouns.
- **Linguistic Analysis:** This stage involves tasks like sentence segmentation, part-of-speech tagging, and stress assignment.
- **Parametric Feature Generation:** Features like pitch, duration, and spectral information are generated based on the analyzed text.
- **Waveform Synthesis:** The final step utilizes these features to create a digital representation of the synthesized speech waveform.

Code Snippet (Example - Simple Text-to-Speech with gTTS in Python):

```python
from gtts import gTTS

# Sample text
text = "This is a sample text to convert to speech."
```

```
# Create a Text-to-Speech object with desired language
tts = gTTS(text=text, lang='en')


# Save the synthesized speech as an audio file
tts.save("sample_speech.mp3")
```

4.4: NLG Techniques: Rule-Based vs. Data-Driven Approaches

Natural Language Generation (NLG) focuses on generating human-like text for various purposes. Here are two main approaches:

- **Rule-Based NLG:** This approach utilizes handcrafted rules and templates to generate text. These rules define how to combine words, phrases, and clauses based on the desired output format and information to be conveyed. This method offers control and explainability but can be time-consuming to develop and maintain for complex tasks.

- **Data-Driven NLG:** This approach leverages machine learning models trained on large amounts of text data. These models learn patterns in how text is structured and used. Techniques like recurrent neural networks (RNNs) and transformers allow for generating more creative and flexible text formats.

Additional Considerations:

- NLG systems often combine elements of both rule-based and data-driven approaches.
- Evaluating NLG systems involves assessing factors like fluency, coherence, grammatical correctness, and how well the generated text meets the desired purpose.

By understanding these speech recognition and NLG techniques, you can appreciate the advancements in enabling natural and interactive communication between humans and machines.

CHAPTER 5

DEEP LEARNING FOR NLP

Deep learning has revolutionized NLP by enabling models to learn complex representations of language from vast amounts of text data. This chapter explores some of the fundamental neural network architectures that power modern NLP applications.

5.1: Introduction to Neural Networks: Perceptrons, Backpropagation

- **Perceptrons:** The building block of neural networks is the perceptron. It is a simple linear model that takes weighted inputs, applies an activation function, and produces an output. These outputs can be binary (classification) or continuous (regression). By combining multiple perceptrons in layers, we create artificial neural networks.

Code Snippet (Example - Perceptron with Sigmoid Activation Function using NumPy):

```python
import numpy as np

# Define a function for the perceptron
def perceptron(x, w, b):
  # Calculate the weighted sum of inputs
  z = np.dot(x, w) + b

  # Apply the sigmoid activation function
  activation = 1 / (1 + np.exp(-z))
  return activation

# Sample input data and weights
x = np.array([1, 0])
w = np.array([0.5, -0.2])
b = 0.3

# Calculate the output of the perceptron
output = perceptron(x, w, b)
print(output)
```

- **Backpropagation:** This is a critical learning algorithm used to train neural networks. It allows the network to adjust its weights based on the difference between its predictions and the actual outputs (error). By iteratively adjusting weights through backpropagation, the network learns to map input data to desired outputs.

5.2: Recurrent Neural Networks (RNNs) for Sequential Data

- **RNNs:** Unlike traditional neural networks, RNNs are designed to handle sequential data like text. They have a loop-like structure where information is passed between layers, allowing the network to consider the context of previous elements when processing the current element. This is crucial for tasks like language translation or text summarization, where the meaning depends on the order of words.

Code Snippet (Example - Simple Vanilla RNN for Character Prediction using TensorFlow):

```
import tensorflow as tf

# Define the RNN model
class RNN(tf.keras.Model):
  def __init__(self, vocab_size, embedding_dim):
```

```python
super(RNN, self).__init__()
        self.embedding = tf.keras.layers.Embedding(vocab_size, embedding_dim)
    self.rnn = tf.keras.layers.SimpleRNN(units=128)
        self.dense = tf.keras.layers.Dense(vocab_size, activation='softmax')

    def call(self, inputs):
    x = self.embedding(inputs)
    x = self.rnn(x)
    output = self.dense(x)
    return output


# Train the model on a character-level dataset (example omitted for brevity)
```

5.3: Long Short-Term Memory (LSTM) Networks

- **LSTMs:** RNNs can struggle with long-term dependencies in sequences. LSTMs address this by introducing memory cells that can store information for longer periods and selectively remember or forget information relevant to the current task. This makes LSTMs particularly powerful for NLP tasks dealing with long sentences or complex relationships between words.

Code Snippet (Example - LSTM for Sentiment Analysis using Keras):

```
from tensorflow.keras.layers import LSTM

# Define the LSTM model for sentiment analysis
model = tf.keras.Sequential([
                tf.keras.layers.Embedding(vocab_size,
embedding_dim),
    LSTM(units=128),
    tf.keras.layers.Dense(1, activation='sigmoid')
])

# Train the model on sentiment-labeled text data
(example omitted for brevity)
```

5.4: Transformers: A Powerful Architecture for NLP Tasks

- **Transformers:** This relatively recent architecture has revolutionized NLP. Unlike RNNs and LSTMs that process data sequentially, Transformers rely on an attention mechanism to learn relationships between all elements in a sequence simultaneously. This allows for efficient parallel processing and has achieved state-of-the-art performance on various NLP tasks like machine translation and question answering.

Understanding these deep learning architectures equips you with the foundational knowledge of how NLP models are built and trained to tackle complex language processing tasks.

CHAPTER 6

NLP FOR REAL-WORLD APPLICATIONS

NLP has transformed how computers interact with the world and revolutionized various industries. This chapter explores some of the exciting real-world applications of NLP.

6.1: Chatbots and Virtual Assistants: Powering Human-Computer Interaction

Chatbots and virtual assistants leverage NLP to enable natural language conversations between humans and machines.

- **Chatbots:** These automated conversational agents can answer user queries, provide customer support, or complete tasks within a specific domain. They use techniques like Natural Language Understanding (NLU) to interpret user questions and Natural Language Generation (NLG) to generate human-like responses. Advancements in NLP enable chatbots to handle complex conversations and personalize interactions.

Code Snippet (Example - Simple Rule-Based Chatbot using Python libraries):

```python
from chatterbot import ChatBot

# Create a chatbot instance
chatbot = ChatBot("My Chatbot")

# Define conversation training data (questions and answers)
conversation = [
  ("Hello", "Hi there! How can I help you today?"),
  ("What is the weather like?", "It's a beautiful day! Enjoy the sunshine."),
  # ... more conversation examples
]

# Train the chatbot on the conversation data
chatbot.train(conversation)

# Start a conversation with the user
```

```
while True:
 user_input = input("You: ")
 if user_input.lower() == "quit":
  break
 bot_response = chatbot.get_response(user_input)
 print("Chatbot:", bot_response)
```

- **Virtual Assistants:** These intelligent agents offer a broader range of features beyond basic conversations. They can integrate with various services, schedule appointments, control smart home devices, and provide personalized assistance. Advanced NLP capabilities enable virtual assistants to understand complex requests and respond in a natural and helpful way.

6.2: Machine Translation: Breaking Down Language Barriers

Machine translation (MT) automatically translates text from one language to another. NLP techniques are crucial for MT systems to understand the semantics, syntax, and cultural nuances of different languages.

- **Statistical Machine Translation (SMT):** This

approach utilizes statistical models trained on large amounts of parallel text data (e.g., English sentences paired with their French translations). The model learns the statistical relationships between words and phrases in different languages to generate translations.

- **Neural Machine Translation (NMT):** This approach leverages deep learning architectures like recurrent neural networks or transformers. NMT models learn complex representations of languages and can generate more fluent and natural-sounding translations compared to traditional SMT approaches.

6.3: Social Media Analysis: Understanding Public Opinion and Trends

Social media analysis utilizes NLP to extract insights from vast amounts of user-generated content on social media platforms.

- **Sentiment Analysis:** NLP helps analyze the sentiment (positive, negative, neutral) expressed in social media posts. This allows brands to understand customer sentiment towards their products or services and gauge public opinion on various topics.

- **Topic Modeling:** NLP techniques like topic modeling can identify the main themes and discussions occurring on social media. This helps businesses track trends, identify emerging customer concerns, and tailor their marketing strategies accordingly.

- **Entity Recognition:** NLP can identify named entities (people, organizations, locations) in social media data. This allows brands to track mentions of their brand or competitors and understand audience demographics and interests.

6.4: NLP in Customer Service: Automating Interactions and Improving Satisfaction

NLP is transforming customer service by enabling automated interactions and enhancing the overall experience.

- **Chatbots for Customer Support:** Chatbots can handle routine customer inquiries, answer frequently asked questions, and provide basic troubleshooting steps. This reduces the burden on human agents and allows them to focus on more complex issues.

- **Sentiment Analysis for Feedback:** Customer reviews and feedback can be analyzed using NLP to identify positive or negative experiences. This helps businesses understand customer satisfaction, identify areas for improvement, and respond to feedback efficiently.

- **Text Summarization for Support Tickets:** NLP can summarize customer support tickets, extracting key information and providing agents with a concise overview of customer issues. This allows for faster resolution and improved efficiency.

By exploring these real-world applications, we witness the transformative power of NLP in shaping human-computer interaction and driving innovation across various industries.

CHAPTER 7

CHALLENGES AND ETHICAL CONSIDERATIONS IN NLP

Despite its remarkable advancements, NLP also faces challenges that require careful consideration. This chapter explores some of the key ethical issues and ongoing discussions in the field.

7.1: Bias and Fairness in NLP Models

NLP models are susceptible to inheriting and amplifying biases present in the data they are trained on. This can lead to unfair or discriminatory outcomes.

- **Data Bias:** If the training data disproportionately reflects certain demographics, genders, or viewpoints, the resulting NLP model might perpetuate those biases. For example, a sentiment analysis model trained on a dataset with mostly negative reviews of female CEOs might classify all reviews of female CEOs as negative, even if the content is neutral or positive.

- **Mitigating Bias:** Techniques like data augmentation (creating more balanced datasets) and fairness-aware machine learning algorithms are being explored to address data bias and promote fairer NLP models.

7.2: Explainability and Interpretability of NLP Systems

Many NLP models, especially deep learning models, can be complex "black boxes" where it's challenging to understand how they arrive at their outputs. This lack of explainability can be problematic:

- **Debugging Errors:** If a model makes a wrong prediction, it's difficult to identify the cause without understanding its reasoning process. This hinders error correction and improvement of the model.
- **Transparency and Trust:** In critical applications like loan approvals or legal decisions, users deserve to understand the rationale behind an NLP-based decision.

7.3: Privacy Concerns in NLP Applications

NLP applications often involve processing sensitive information like user conversations or social media posts.

This raises privacy concerns:

- **Data Collection and Storage:** Protecting user privacy necessitates anonymizing data or obtaining explicit consent before collecting and storing personal information for NLP tasks.
- **Security and Data Leaks:** Robust security measures are crucial to prevent unauthorized access to sensitive data processed by NLP systems.

7.4: The Future of NLP: Responsible Development and Deployment

As NLP continues to evolve, responsible development and deployment are essential:

- **Mitigating Bias:** Researchers and developers must actively work towards building fairer and unbiased NLP models through responsible data collection and algorithm design.
- **Explainable AI:** Efforts in explainable AI (XAI) research aim to develop techniques that make NLP models more transparent and interpretable, fostering trust and understanding.
- **Privacy-Preserving NLP:** Techniques like federated

learning and differential privacy can enable NLP tasks on decentralized data, minimizing the need for centralized data storage and enhancing user privacy.

By addressing these challenges and prioritizing ethical considerations, the future of NLP holds immense potential to benefit society and empower humans with advanced language understanding capabilities.

CHAPTER 8

NLP for Developers: Tools and Libraries

This chapter dives into the practical aspects of implementing NLP techniques. We'll explore essential tools and libraries that empower developers to build and deploy NLP applications.

8.1: Popular NLP Libraries: TensorFlow, PyTorch, Deep Learning Frameworks

Deep learning frameworks like TensorFlow and PyTorch are powerful tools for building and training NLP models. They provide:

- **Tensor Operations:** Efficient manipulation of multidimensional arrays (tensors) that form the foundation of deep learning models.

- **Neural Network Layers:** Pre-built components like convolutional layers, recurrent layers, and attention mechanisms commonly used in NLP architectures.

- **Optimization Algorithms:** Tools to train models by adjusting parameters to minimize errors and improve performance.

Code Snippet (Example - Simple Sentiment Analysis Model with TensorFlow):

```
from tensorflow.keras.layers import Embedding, LSTM, Dense

# Define the sentiment analysis model
model = tf.keras.Sequential([
  Embedding(vocab_size, embedding_dim),
  LSTM(units=128),
  Dense(1, activation='sigmoid')
])

# Compile the model with optimizer and loss function
model.compile(loss='binary_crossentropy', optimizer='adam', metrics=['accuracy'])

# Train the model on labeled sentiment data (example omitted for brevity)
```

8.2: Pre-trained Language Models: Utilizing Existing Knowledge

Pre-trained language models (PLMs) are powerful NLP

models trained on massive amounts of text data. They learn rich representations of language that can be fine-tuned for specific tasks. Popular PLMs include:

- **BERT:** Bidirectional Encoder Representations from Transformers, known for its ability to understand the context of words in a sentence.
- **GPT-3:** Generative Pre-trained Transformer 3, known for its impressive capabilities in text generation and creative writing tasks.

Code Snippet (Example - Text Classification with Fine-tuned BERT using Hugging Face Transformers):

```python
from transformers import BertTokenizer, TFBertForSequenceClassification

# Load pre-trained BERT model and tokenizer
tokenizer = BertTokenizer.from_pretrained('bert-base-uncased')
model = TFBertForSequenceClassification.from_pretrained('bert-base-uncased', num_labels=2)

# Tokenize text and prepare input for the model
text = "This movie was a total disappointment."
```

```
encoded_text = tokenizer(text, return_tensors='tf')

# Predict sentiment using the fine-tuned BERT model
predictions = model(encoded_text)
predicted_class                              =
tf.argmax(predictions.logits).numpy()[0]

# Interpret the prediction (class labels need to be
defined)
if predicted_class == 0:
  print("Sentiment: Positive")
else:
  print("Sentiment: Negative")
```

8.3: Building and Training NLP Pipelines

An NLP pipeline is a sequence of steps that process raw text data and extract meaningful information. Here are common stages in an NLP pipeline:

1. **Text Preprocessing:** Cleaning and preparing the text data by tasks like tokenization (splitting text into words), normalization (lowercasing, removing punctuation), and stemming/lemmatization (reducing words to their base form).

2. **Feature Engineering:** Creating numerical representations of text data suitable for machine

learning models. Techniques like word embedding (mapping words to vectors) are often used.

3. **Model Training:** Training an NLP model on labeled data appropriate for the desired task (e.g., sentiment analysis, named entity recognition).

4. **Evaluation:** Assessing the performance of the trained model on unseen data using metrics like accuracy, precision, recall, or F1-score.

5. **Prediction:** Applying the trained model to new, unlabeled text data to generate predictions or perform the desired NLP task.

8.4: Debugging and Evaluating NLP Models

Developing effective NLP models is an iterative process. Here are key aspects of debugging and evaluation:

- **Error Analysis:** Examining incorrect predictions of the model to identify patterns and understand where it's struggling. Techniques like visualizing attention weights in transformer models can provide insights.

- **Data Augmentation:** Improving the training data by techniques like generating synthetic data or oversampling underrepresented classes can enhance model robustness.

- **Hyperparameter Tuning:** Adjusting model parameters like learning rate or number of neurons can significantly impact performance. Grid search or random search techniques can be used for efficient hyperparameter tuning.

Additional Tools and Libraries:

- **spaCy:** A popular Python library for various NLP tasks like tokenization, part-of-speech tagging, named entity recognition, and dependency parsing.

- **NLTK:** The Natural Language Toolkit, a comprehensive Python library for NLP tasks, including text processing, classification, and machine learning.

- **Keras:** A high-level deep learning API built on top of TensorFlow, offering a user-friendly interface for building and training neural networks.

- **Gensim:** A Python library for topic modeling, document similarity, and other tasks related to natural language processing.

- **Scikit-learn:** While not exclusively for NLP, scikit-learn offers valuable tools for data preprocessing, feature engineering, and machine learning algorithms that can be integrated into NLP pipelines.

8.5: Conclusion: Building a Future with NLP

The field of NLP is rapidly evolving, and the tools and libraries mentioned above are just a starting point. By leveraging these resources, developers can build innovative NLP applications that bridge the gap between human and machine communication. As we address the challenges and prioritize responsible development, NLP has the potential to revolutionize various aspects of our lives, from communication and information retrieval to creative content generation and personalized experiences.

This chapter has equipped you with a foundational understanding of NLP concepts, techniques, and the essential tools developers utilize to build and deploy NLP applications. The future of NLP is bright, and by staying involved and exploring these advancements, you can contribute to shaping a future where humans and machines collaborate seamlessly using the power of language.

CHAPTER 9

NLP in the Future: Emerging Trends and Advancements

The field of NLP is constantly pushing boundaries and exploring new possibilities. This chapter delves into some of the exciting trends and advancements shaping the future of NLP.

9.1: Multimodal NLP: Integrating Text with Speech and Vision

Traditional NLP focuses primarily on textual data. Multimodal NLP expands on this by incorporating other modalities like speech and vision to create a more comprehensive understanding of language.

- **Speech-enabled NLP:** Combining speech recognition and NLP allows for tasks like real-time conversation translation, voice-based search with natural language queries, and improved accessibility for visually impaired users.

- **Vision-enabled NLP:** Integrating computer vision with NLP enables applications like image captioning (generating descriptions of images), visual question answering (answering questions based on images), and scene understanding (extracting meaning from visual content).

Code Snippet (Example - Simple Image Captioning with TensorFlow and Keras):

```python
from tensorflow.keras.applications import VGG16
from tensorflow.keras.layers import Dense, LSTM, Embedding, TimeDistributed

# Load a pre-trained image feature extractor (VGG16)
image_model = VGG16(weights='imagenet', include_top=False)

# Define the NLP model with an LSTM for caption generation
text_model = tf.keras.Sequential([
  Embedding(vocab_size, embedding_dim),
  LSTM(units=256, return_sequences=True),
              TimeDistributed(Dense(vocab_size, activation='softmax'))
  ])
```

```
# Combine the models for image captioning (example
omitted for brevity)
```

9.2: Generative NLP: Creating Human-Quality Text and Code

Generative NLP models can create human-quality text formats like poems, code, scripts, musical pieces, and more. This opens doors for various creative and practical applications.

- **Text Generation:** Models like GPT-3 can generate realistic and creative text formats, fostering applications like automated writing assistance, content creation, or even chatbot development with more natural and engaging conversations.

- **Code Generation:** Generative models are being explored to assist programmers by automatically generating code snippets or completing code based on natural language instructions.

Code Snippet (Example - Text Generation with GPT-2 using Hugging Face Transformers):

```
from transformers import TextGenerator

# Load a pre-trained text generation model
text_generator = TextGenerator.from_pretrained("gpt2")

# Generate text starting with a prompt
prompt = "Once upon a time, there was a brave knight..."
generated_text = text_generator(prompt, max_length=100, temperature=0.7)

print(generated_text.sequences[0])
```

9.3: NLP for Low-Resource Languages: Bridging the Digital Divide

Most NLP research focuses on high-resource languages like English. NLP for low-resource languages aims to bridge the digital divide by developing techniques that work effectively with limited data available for these languages.

- **Transfer Learning:** Leveraging knowledge from pre-trained models on high-resource languages and adapting them to low-resource languages can improve performance by mitigating data scarcity.

- **Data Augmentation Techniques:** Techniques like back-translation (translating text to a high-resource language and then back to the low-resource language) can be used to create synthetic data and improve model training on low-resource languages.

9.4: The Future of Human-Computer Interaction: More Natural and Fluid Communication

NLP advancements are leading to a future where human-computer interaction (HCI) becomes more natural and fluid.

- **Conversational AI:** NLP is crucial for developing intelligent conversational agents that can understand complex user queries, respond in a natural and engaging way, and personalize interactions across different domains.

- **Augmented Reality (AR) and Virtual Reality (VR):** NLP can enable real-time language translation and integration of natural language interactions within AR/VR experiences, fostering more immersive and interactive environments.

By exploring these emerging trends, we gain insights into the transformative potential of NLP in shaping the future of communication and interaction between humans and machines. As NLP continues to evolve, we can expect even more groundbreaking advancements that will redefine how we live, work, and interact with technology.

CHAPTER 10

THE POWER OF NLP IN A CONNECTED WORLD

This concluding chapter reflects on the transformative impact of NLP, explores exciting future directions, and emphasizes the importance of responsible innovation in this rapidly evolving field.

10.1: The Impact of NLP on Society and Business

NLP has permeated various aspects of our lives, shaping society and business in profound ways:

- **Enhanced Communication and Accessibility:** NLP empowers people with disabilities through speech recognition and text-to-speech technologies, fosters real-time translation across languages, and breaks down communication barriers.

- **Personalized Experiences:** NLP personalized user experiences across various domains.

Recommendation systems leverage NLP to suggest relevant products or content, chatbots provide tailored customer support, and intelligent virtual assistants anticipate user needs.

- **Data-Driven Decision Making:** NLP empowers businesses to extract insights from vast amounts of text data, like customer reviews, social media conversations, or market research reports. This enables data-driven decision making and helps businesses understand customer sentiment, identify trends, and optimize their strategies.

- **Revolutionizing Industries:** NLP is transforming various industries. In healthcare, NLP facilitates medical record analysis and automates tasks, while in finance, it empowers fraud detection and risk assessment through document processing and sentiment analysis of financial news.

10.2: The Future of NLP Research and Development

The future of NLP research holds immense potential for

groundbreaking advancements:

- **Explainable AI (XAI) for NLP:** Research in XAI aims to develop more interpretable NLP models. This will enhance trust and transparency in their decision-making processes, especially for critical applications.

- **Lifelong Learning NLP Systems:** Developing NLP models that continuously learn and adapt from new data streams will enable continuous improvement and real-world adaptability.

- **Dialogue Systems with Reasoning and Commonsense Knowledge:** NLP systems that incorporate reasoning and commonsense knowledge will be able to engage in more natural and comprehensive conversations, understanding context and implications beyond literal meaning.

- **NLP for Human-Robot Collaboration:** As robots become more integrated into our lives, NLP will be crucial for enabling seamless communication and collaboration between humans and robots.

10.3: A Call for Responsible Innovation in NLP

As NLP continues to evolve, responsible development and deployment are paramount:

- **Bias Mitigation:** Researchers and developers must actively address bias in NLP models to ensure fairness and inclusivity. This requires diverse datasets, careful model design, and continuous monitoring and mitigation strategies.

- **Privacy Protection:** Robust privacy-preserving techniques are essential to protect user data used in NLP applications. Techniques like federated learning and differential privacy can help achieve this.

- **Human-in-the-Loop NLP:** NLP should augment human capabilities, not replace them. Responsible development should focus on building human-centered NLP systems that empower humans and promote collaboration.

10.4: Conclusion: The Journey of Unlocking Human Language for Machines

This book has explored the fascinating world of NLP, from its fundamental concepts to cutting-edge applications. NLP unlocks the power of human language for machines, enabling them to understand, interpret, and interact with the world in a more meaningful way. As we move forward, responsible innovation in NLP will be crucial to harness its full potential for the benefit of society. The journey of unlocking human language for machines is far from over, and the exciting advancements to come hold the promise of a future where communication between humans and machines becomes more natural, seamless, and empowering.

ABOUT THE AUTHOR

Writer's Bio:

 Benjamin Evans, a respected figure in the tech world, is known for his insightful commentary and analysis. With a strong educational background likely in fields such as computer science, engineering, or business, he brings a depth of knowledge to his discussions on emerging technologies and industry trends. Evans' knack for simplifying complex concepts, coupled with his innate curiosity and passion for innovation, has established him as a go-to source for understanding the dynamics of the digital landscape. Through articles, speeches, and social media, he shares his expertise and offers valuable insights into the impact of technology on society.

www.ingramcontent.com/pod-product-compliance
Lightning Source LLC
LaVergne TN
LVHW051608050326
832903LV00033B/4398